THE DAY AFTER

JUNETEENTH

DJELI

DREAMCATCHER
ENTERTAINMENT, LLC

Brattleboro, VT

CONTENTS

INTRODUCTION

Juneteenth: is the oldest nationally celebrated commemoration of the ending of slavery in the United States.

From its Galveston, Texas origin in 1865, the observance of June 19th as the African American Emancipation Day has spread across the United States and beyond.

About The day after Juneteenth:

A few years ago on the day after a Juneteenth celebration I sat in deep contemplation. My contemplation was filled with curiosity and tinged with sorrow. I wondered what those enslaved men, women and children in Texas felt after hearing of their freedom. What went through their minds when they discovered it took more than two years for the report of their liberation to reach them?

What is freedom to someone who has never known freedom? If you are born with chains on your feet, chains on your wrists and chains on your heart and that is all you have ever known, what happens when the chains that have defined a good portion of your existence are no longer present? Who are you? Who do you become? If the entirety of your life has existed inside of a box and the ones who have confined you have reinforced that all that is outside of the that box is dangerous or deadly and you haven't the means to handle anything on the outside, then liberation suddenly looks like a death sentence. The freedom afforded these formerly enslaved people can be more fearful than the uncertainty of enslavement. New skill sets must be learned in order to survive. New ways of being must come into awareness.

The writings contained within these pages are a result of my living with these questions more than a century and a half after the first Juneteenth celebration.

Son rise

I cast my vision in the darkness,
Straining to to make tangible
the formless blackness before me
That I unintentionally project upon the shadow wall
All that I hide deep within
Taking every ounce of strength I have to fight the panic
The longer I stare the more I see
The unwanted emotion trapped within me
The unreal wrapped in shadow
Emboldened by night
Threatens my being
Encouraging me to extinguish my light
Extinguish my light
I will not comply
Without the light hope will die
I will not fight
I will lovingly feed darkness my light
I will not stand on this ground
Full well knowing it belongs to no man
I will walk
I will sit
I will make a joyful sound
I cast my vision in the darkness
I project my light
Like the sun licking the horizon to kiss the night
the new day dawns
Putting hope in sight
I live another day
I breathe another breath
I see my children grow
I watch my daughter rise.
I watch my sons rise.

May I...

May I live on this piece of land?
If history serves, my life won't be long
I'm not asking to own it, cause all land is free
I would like a place to lay my head
To cast off the chains that have bound and sought to
control me

Great Granddad never got his forty acres and a mule
He was set loose yet never set free
I'm sure he'd like me to collect the debt that is owed
And I know 'cause I've been told this land ain't free
What I ask for is what is owed by his legacy surviving to
me

May I live on this piece of land?
When the people arrived and put stakes in the ground
Who did they pay for the land that now is not free?
When the people put up fences that contained enslaved
people that looked a great deal like me
Is that when the land became suddenly not free?

May I live on this piece of land? Please?
Regardless of where I stray or how far I roam
This piece of land keeps calling me, calling me home
The rivers nearby converge
Spring transformation is wrought
This land remains not to be sold not to be bought
To be lived on
To be loved on
May I live on this piece of land? Please?

It ain't safe yet,

Step inside,
There is work to be done,
Step inside,
I said there is work to be done,
How black are you?
Blue black? True black?
And how do you know?
When you speak what words fall out?
And how hard do you have work to lay out the words the world
can hear?
Are you ready to defend your blackness?
Cause you gonna have to.
There is no pass, never was one unless you can pass for not being
one.
Step inside
Your soul ain't ready yet.
Your heart is too tender and would make a tasty tar-tar
Your line is not strong enough for you to balance upon as you try
to rise above
To hold up, to bring up,
 the ones you love.
Your mind is too small it needs to become a universe
Only then will you truly have a place that is safe.
Step inside
Grow yourself, not your ego
so immense your body can not contain you
Grow your roots
So deep that nothing of this world could possibly unearth you
That no one word,
That no one paragraph
That no one document
Could ever knock you off your center
Grow your mind
That your wisdom shows without the utterance of a word

That your knowledge is attached to every planet of existence
That you know there is no longer anything worth fighting for
That you know the winner of the war still has enemies
That you know peace
That you know peace
That you know..... peace
Then and only then will it be safe to step outside.

Oops

I messed up
I thought we could be friends
And you thought we could be friends
You told me about that thing that made us both laugh,
We have so much in common
I had a dog growing up
And so did you
I washed dishes in the same chain restaurant that you did
We both hated working in that fast food joint
We have so much in common
We both graduated a semester early
Neither of us wants to go back to where we grew up
Although we loved growing up there
We have the same taste in women
Or so I thought
Until I pointed out the cute family in the park
And you were disgusted that the children were mutts
You wondered "how are we ever gonna know who we are when
we got mixed breeds running the streets?"
I thought we could be friends
So I picked up my jaw
I wondered had you even noticed my milk chocolate skin?
Have you noticed the beautiful Grade A dark amber children of
mine?
I am different you say
I'm not like the…. Stop!
what I am is tired of that trite line of reasoning.
What I am is silent no more
Oh, we can be friends when you kick those old tired ways out the
door
I messed up
I thought we could be friends
But I love myself too much for that.

Too much to live for

If you find my lifeless body hanging from a tree,
Know that I have too much to live for,
I am not a fruit that easily grows on trees,
Yet too many trees have fruit that looks like me,
and too many Mamas sobbing hard on their knees,
Knowing that their baby had so much to live for,
Jemima is not my aunt,
Ben is not my uncle,
If you are too busy fighting to keep your belly full
That you have no time to fight to keep my lungs full
I have to let you go
because I have too much to live for,
There is nothing about my blackness that I need to hide,
So you best believe if I'm hanging it was not suicide,
So hear what I'm saying
cause I say it with pride
I have too much to live for.

It still ain't safe

Get in the ditch
Master 's a coming
Get in the ditch
I see lights ahead
It ain't right to be dark after dark
Unless you are playing or singing
Making it easier for the man to drink the sauce that enables him to
ease the pain of putting such a hurt on our people
Get in the ditch
Our presence reminds them of the other side of the coin.
Don't stay in the ditch
Let your muscles grow stronger each time you pull yourself out.
Don't stay in the ditch
Look around you, this is the promised land
Don't stay in the ditch
The time will come where you need to be seen
The time will come where you need to be heard
Don't stay in the ditch
When you rise to power
Remember the ditch is a place for no one man, woman or child
Get out of the ditch and remember this
When you rise to power

Declaration

We hold these truths to be self evident that all humans are not created equal,
Some have been created with more
while some have been created with less
Some are rewarded in life while some are barred from success,
We hold these truths to be self evident that all lives matter
although some matter less.
We are all entitled to life, liberty and the pursuit of happiness,
Unless it is determined by majority decision that you are not,
The pursuit of happiness is for all
until the powers that be decide that rules do not apply to everyone,
Yet those rules will apply to everyone in accordance to how they react to the sun.
Life is only fair if you are fair
In all fairness you will fair less if you lack fairness,
So great is the sin to lack fairness of skin
That all rules must be laid by
By show of darkness
You must be prepared to accept less
So be it known that only some were created in the image of God.
And you know who you are
after all why would God create your defective bod?
We hold these truths to be self evident
In God we trust.

I am created in the image of God
Therefore when God looks in the mirror
It is my image that is reflected
I have no delusion of grandeur
God has no delusion of insignificance.

Clarity

Inhale, exhale,
Longing to become the air I breathe,
Wash away the color that divides me,
From others who are not the same color,
Clear my thought of fear
Breathe in the air
That changes me from all I am, to clear,
My hands are wet
From washing away the scars the chains have left
From generations held enslaved
The air dries the wet from my hands
From the pain of my ancestors I am saved
Inhale, exhale,
The air washes clear my mind,
To sleep I must go
To sleep I must go
When I wake,
I will have left this all behind.

More questions

How is it I can be discontent with who I am today?
Yet adore who I was yesterday?
And fully know that the same will be true tomorrow?
That flawed yester - me found the path that led me to this now
And in hindsight is not as flawed as I perceive the present me to
be
I am recognizing my train of thinking is mostly missing the station
And quite possibly needs uncoupling from the ideas it takes as
fuel

The breeze

Winds blow
Carrying birdsong
Grasshopper, cricket, cicada symphonette
Sun's rays illuminate
fingers of divinity casting forth
Eyes closed
Revealing the unsee-able
Awakening senses
Far too long asleep
Clarity of vision
Concealing the known
Revealing the unknown
Eyes open
Winds blow
All becomes invisible
Except what is expected

Do I approve of the use of violence?

In order to answer the question I have questions to ask.
If I dragged the ocean how many bones would I find still bound in chains?
Would all the black bodies hung from trees exceed all the white women drowned, burned and stoned as witches?
Why did you stop killing the white women?
Is shooting a black child for wearing a hoodie violent?
I guess I first have to understand what you consider violence.
So let me clarify with some questions?
If I do to you what you have done to me, is that violent?
But what you do to me is justified?
If a white man shoots up a school and kills white children is that violence or mental instability?
If a black woman, man or child asks a white person to stop killing our people is that violence?
Is the asking reason enough to shoot?
Is the standing silently hoping that the violence stops, violence?
Let me get this clear
You want to know if I approve of the use of violence?
Are you asking if I mind your beating me?
Are you asking if I will lie down so that you may kneel on my neck?
Are you asking if I am willing to stand in front of the bullet you put in your gun with my name on it?
Are you asking If I am willing to turn my back while you stop my mother, father, sister, brother from breathing another breath?
So,
Do I approve of the use of violence?
If that is the language you speak,
I am willing to speak to you in your language,
I have a question for you,
Will you please listen?

I have another question,
Will you listen, please?
Oh,
To answer your question,
Shut up and listen.

Sit down

Sit down
It's alright to rest a moment
You fought the fight when no one else knew what you were
fighting
You've built your muscle by walking strong through storms that
others did not weather,
Sit down
The living you've lived is like no other
And millions more can tell similar tales
You grew strong when you heard what was said and you did not
breathe fire
Sit down
You've been brave
Showing up when only you looked like you
And your parents before you were brave yet could not share all
they went through
You smiled when the tornado of razor blades was cutting you on
the inside
You showed up when you didn't want to but you had to
So now I invite you to sit down
Not because you earned it
Because you are worth it
Because you loving you sometimes looks like sitting down
Go on now,
Sit down
God is working miracles

On Gratitude

For a time my silence was necessary as I needed everything to wash over me and through me. I needed to hear the words of kindness and love and accept that I was worthy of their speaking. I needed to hear the words of pain and discomfort and know that I need not react, and know that I could listen without judgement. I needed to sit in my silent discomfort and understand the discomfort as learning. I needed to grow in the strength of silence. I needed not only to hear what was spoken but also to hear what was unspoken. I learned to accept the silence to be as adept a teacher as the cacophony. In the process I also needed to restore trust and love in self.

The lesson in progress is that the love I have for anyone and anything is the divine love that flows through me reflected back to me. I found in the silence the ability to fill to my fullest in love allowing love to flow into the world. I am grateful for the teachers, the students and student teachers that have aided this discovery. I am grateful for the companions that have compassionately been at hand as I stumbled and regained my stance, as I tripped and restored my stride while I mostly un-masterfully acquired and learned to use the tools I have today. I am grateful for the knowledge that love does not look the way it once did. I am grateful for the knowledge that being loved and loving are entitled me from before birth.

You are reading this because I am grateful for the presence you have had in this lesson of life and love.

#122742063018

I was born to be a prostitute,
I knew this was who I would be when
Grandmama walked ten miles to clean houses seven days a week.
I knew this is who I would be when
Great Grandma died and the family inherited the burden of
putting her in the ground and putting food on the table.
I knew this is who I would be when
My body started to change and the tickle fights got messy.
The boys started acting like men and the men started treating me
like fruit
I knew this is who I would be when
The men bruised my flesh and it was my fault for being too fine,
too cute
I knew this is who I would be when
I first heard the darker the fruit the sweeter the juice
I knew this is who I would be when
I cried for help and they cleaned me up so my hurters could have
a second helping
I knew this is who I would be when
I cried for help and I was reassured that love is like that some times
I knew this is who I would be when
I shot the man who hurt me and no one cared why
And I was sentenced to die
And no one could see that I was broken
Swept into the corner with no words spoken
The coffee stain on the coffee table
A nuisance easily covered with a coaster
I was born to be a prostitute for your pleasure
Grandmama was born with nothing and died with less
The least I can do is lift my dress
And maybe I can leave my babies something to forget me with
I was born to be a prostitute
When Grandmama walked ten miles home to cook and clean for
her own.

When Grandma died and there was no one left to see how brilliant
my mind is
When the men started touching me and I liked that someone
could see me
When I stopped hearing the word love and no one seemed to
miss it.
I was born to be a prostitute when he hit me.
He hit me. He hit me
When I made him stop, they gave me this number,
It sure does seem like the world needs a prostitute.

I am not your nigger

I am not your nigger
Nigger. Nigger. Nigger.
Nigger only exists in your mind
When your mind fractured
into believing there is white
And there is other
When you embraced white
and had no conceivable use for the other
The nigger was born
And born only in your mind
The white side of your mind decided it should
Cleave the shadow side of your mind and send it packing
Yet the shadow still remained
Your mind in its inability to do anything
Thrust the cleaving to the body
Very soon after cleaving started you realized it was not self
sustaining to cleave oneself
And much easier to cleave others
So the nigger side of your mind leapt through your mind to
someone in cleavable proximity
Let it be clear
The nigger is your mind's baby
And all the while smuggly in the shadow of your mind safely sits
your nigger mind baby smiling
The injustice of it all
For every nigger you kill in the world
One will always live on in your mind…. nigger
So know that you can't remove from the world what only lives in
your mind
In essence you are what is of your mind
Therefore, you are what you know you are
And the reason I use the "N" word
I am not your nigger

Dance

Dance the dance of oceans
Undulate, flow,
Dance the dance of knowledge
Let your wisdom show
Dance the dance of life
Let your light shine on and on
Dance the dance of love
Until all your fear is gone
Dance the dance of patience
For this is your life to live
Cast your gaze upon the ocean
That's where all eternity waits for you
Stand on the the shore and wait no more
And let the water come to you.

PTSTOP

Why is it called "post" traumatic?
When this is perpetual trauma
Every day you bring up Trayvon, and George and Breonna and all,
It is real, in real time and right now,
Go home to your reality show, your game show, your streaming
binge, your online gaming
While I go home ....and shut that down
I am so tired of the hurt
Reminding me of how much I hurt does not make the hurt less
I have the freedom to go wherever I want
But not the freedom to belong wherever I am
Please tell me where my people were stolen from?
Please tell me what ship my ancestors were on when they landed
here?
Please tell me this is all a bad dream
Please tell me... cause I'm 'bout to scream
Again
I know you haven't heard me scream
'cause I know better.... I go where y'all can't hear
'cause my emotions are offensive
Black rage
The reason so many brothers like me are in a cage

I've manage to keep my voice down, hold back the yell
This body, this mind would lose it in a cell
I long to take my shoes off and feel the land
Be it forest floor or beach sand
Take my shoes off no more to roam
let the land caress my feet and call me home
A home were I can fully feel
So I can shed this armor and fully heal
So sore to my core from this persistent stress
Sleep I must find
So much need for rest
Tomorrow it all begins again
Until those in comfort say STOP

Where

Where does my blackness end and I begin?
I may know the answer but do you?
My blackness is the price the republic places on my person.
And I know my value to be so much more
Eyes wide open I can see
There is a curse upon us
Eyes shut fast I can see
There is a curse upon us all
Raise your hand as high as you can reach
Is it a black hand you raised?
Or is it a white hand?
Look upon the person next to you on your right
Look upon the person next to you on your left
Are they Black?
Or are they White?
What is their value?
What are they worth?
Are they worth more than you? Or less?
With each question asked
Where does your comfort end?
For this person's life how much would you spend?
There is a curse upon us

Until you stop being white
And I stop being black
This curse upon us will have no end.

The universe

The great big oneness
Ever expanding and contracting
Never seeking only finding
Undivided
So often the answers sought by fracturing
When the wholeness is the truth
God is the diminutive of Goddess
For the god only exist by lessening
Woman is the whole and man the derivative
Man is the planet that lives within the universe of woman
A portion of the whole
All that is man is an extract of the woman
For He does not exist without She
Therefore man must divide to gain importance
until we all embrace our unity
Goddess, Woman, Universe, womb of creation
Divine one-ness is our birthright
Ever expanding and contracting
Embracing the universe

Black is love

Standing with my Brothers and Sisters
Finally home,
Healing in process,
Remembering self
Remembering soul,
Loving with my Brothers and Sisters,
United in individuality
Connected by love
Understanding the universe within,
No matter what is added
The Blackness remains
No matter how much is taken away
The Blackness remains
Here we stand
Here we sit
In the glory of Blackness,
In love.

Un-fragile

We are the first snowflakes of the blizzard,
We are the embers that keep the fire alive,
We are the unspoken words of our ancestors,
That need to be heard,
We are the embodiment of loving ourselves in order to love the
world,
Our faces are the faces of the universe,
We are the song of unity
We are the song of unity
Come as you are
This is your community
This is our community
Speaking our truth
Abundant truth
Speaking our love
Abundant love

Re minding Black Joy

A year of joy or a lifetime of joy
Gathered together
Ever changing
The sounds and songs of the elders cutting through lifetimes and
lifetimes
Blessing the blooms in Claire's garden
(mmmm)
The iris scent
Nourishment with my love
Wholesomeness without looking over my shoulder
Listen now
Listen now
The drums of Africa beat within
Let the cougars lovingly roam
And we dance
And we dance
We are the joy that I have searched for
we are the medicine that makes us whole
We are the joy
Rest now
You are home
I am home
I am home

The Ancestors breath

Bones unearthed so roads may go places
Our people were not permitted to know,
Rise up, open up, open up,
The medicine is in the land,
Is in the mangoes,
Is in the yams,
The ancestors words are on the wind,
The shamanic gifts are in my bones,
Our inheritance, our sense, our skill,
We are blessed by the sharing,
We are blessed with ancestral gifts,
Just you being here is an act of defiance,
I see you
I see you with God's eye,
I breathe you in with my ancestors' breath.

Declaration of interconnectedness

(The narrator speaks "I declare that" the crowd in unison responds " we are one")

I declare that we are one
Every father's daughter
Every mother's son
I declare that we are one
We are all human
There is no race
So why must I run?
I declare that we are one
We need to restore the joy to living
Cause hatin's playing with a loaded gun
I declare that we are one
Until this mantra flows from every mouth
There is work to be done
I declare that we are one
Rise up, Rise up
Look around
Brother to sister to sister to brother
To Auntie and Uncle to cousin
We must value one another
It must be repeated
I declare that we are one
It must be repeated
It must be sung
Until it rings throughout the world
Like church bells rung

I declare that we are one
Emancipate your mind
Let past hurts be undone
As the mountains grow
And the rivers run
I declare that we are one
I declare that we are one
I declare that we are one.

ABOUT THE AUTHOR

Djeli is a story weaver who helps transform overwhelm to overjoy for people of all ages and backgrounds. Ki is a thought leader, life coach, public speaker, lifelong storyteller, and former Cirque du Soleil acrobat who has traveled the world collecting stories. Having to heal from a physical injury introduced Djeli to the need for healthy healing practices through story weaving. Ki believes that we are all each other's medicine. Djeli's background of growing up on a farm in South Jersey created a true connection to nature. Through the story weaving process, ki hopes to help others discover how their own connection to nature affects their personal stories.

Djeli's stories are designed to promote healing for individuals hurting from the problems of the world. Ki believes that no matter where we travel in the world, we laugh and cry in the same language. Ki uses oral and written traditions, including poetry, to create an atmosphere of curiosity and dialogue, even around difficult topics. Djeli's open and honest approach of speaking from the heart helps others breathe life into their own stories as part of a healing process.

Djeli can be reached at:
Email: info@iamdjeli.com
Website: https://iamdjeli.com/
Facebook: **https://www.facebook.com/billosophy101**
Instagram: @billosophy101

Made in the USA
Middletown, DE
04 November 2023

41793295R00022